I0484002

WORKING CONDITIONS AND FACTORY AUDITING IN THE CHINESE TOY INDUSTRY

HEARING

BEFORE THE

CONGRESSIONAL-EXECUTIVE COMMISSION ON CHINA

ONE HUNDRED THIRTEENTH CONGRESS

SECOND SESSION

DECEMBER 11, 2014

Printed for the use of the Congressional-Executive Commission on China

Available via the World Wide Web: http://www.cecc.gov

U.S. GOVERNMENT PUBLISHING OFFICE

92–632 PDF   WASHINGTON : 2015

CONTENTS

WORKING CONDITIONS AND FACTORY AUDITING IN THE CHINESE TOY INDUSTRY

THURSDAY, DECEMBER 11, 2014

Congressional-Executive
Commission on China,
Washington, DC.

The hearing was convened, pursuant to notice, at 10:46 a.m., in Room SVC 212–10, Capitol Visitor's Center, Hon. Sherrod Brown, Chairman, presiding.

OPENING STATEMENT OF HON. SHERROD BROWN, A U.S. SENATOR FROM OHIO; CHAIRMAN, CONGRESSIONAL–EXECUTIVE COMMISSION ON CHINA

Chairman BROWN. The Commission will come to order. Thank you all for joining us, the five of you. I appreciate that very much. I am sorry for the lateness of the start.

We just had a vote on the Senate floor and there are House votes going on, too, so colleagues, including Cochairman Smith, I believe, will be joining us. We will have people kind of coming in and out. I apologize for the unevenness of that and what that sometimes does to hearings here.

This is an important hearing. This is the last hearing that I will preside over with a change in the majority in the Senate. Chairman Smith and I have worked together for four years in this Commission taking turns chairing.

The chair next year will go back to the House and the Cochair will be a Senate Republican. It has been an honor to work with this Commission for these almost four years.

David Machinist, today, thank you for the work that you did on this, Paul and Lawrence, especially as the two Staff Directors, for the work they have done on this. Lawrence is moving on and I am particularly appreciative for the close personal relationship and the work that we have been able to do together.

This hearing is important and fitting because of the time of the year it is. Obviously, this is when many of the toys that are made in China are purchased in the United States for the holiday season.

I have three grandchildren. I know the excitement of the holidays and I know what these toys mean to children and parents and grandchildren. Not just should we care about the quality and the safety of the toys and issues like lead paint, we should also care about the workers—something we don't think much about on Christmas mornings or holiday mornings or when we look at these toys, think about the people who actually make these toys.

It used to be the case that toys were made in America, often by union workers, often by workers that could actually afford to buy the toys that they make. I remember some years ago after NAFTA [North American Free Trade Agreement] passed, at my own expense, I flew to the Texas-Mexican border and went across the border with a friend and went to an auto plant in Mexico.

It was new. It looked like an auto plant in Lorain, Ohio or Avon Lake, Ohio or Cleveland, Ohio. It was modern. It was clean. The workers were working hard. There was one difference between the two auto plants, the Mexican one and the Ohio one and that is the Mexican one did not have a parking lot because the workers could not afford to buy the cars that they were making.

We see much of that in the toy industry. So often workers cannot afford to, for their children, buy the toys that they make.

Towns like Bryan, Ohio, a little town in the northwest corner of Ohio, near to Indiana and to Michigan—Bryan, Ohio—for years workers at the company called the Ohio Art Company made something that most of you, if you grew up in this country would have played with, something called Etch-A-Sketch. A decade or so ago, Walmart came to the Ohio Art Company and said, we want to sell your Etch-A-Sketch, your product for under $10 at Walmart.

The Ohio Art Company thought they had no choice and they shut down production, most of their production in the United States, moved it to China where they could produce with low-wage workers and a whole lot of other things, could produce these toys and Walmart could make the money that they thought they should make from each toy.

Today the production of Etch-A-Sketch is now in Shenzhen, China. A hundred people lost their jobs and a community, in part, lost some of its pride when that happened.

Today, some 85 percent of our toys come from China. They will be made by factory workers like the ones investigated in China Labor Watch's most recent report. Some are temporary workers, some are students, some make as little as $1.23 an hour, some work more than 100 hours of overtime a month, in blatant violation of China's overtime laws. China's laws are not all that bad, but the enforcement of those laws is.

These young people often live in crowded dorms, sometimes 18 people to a room. They stand for long hours at work. Emergency exit doors are locked. We have seen the tragedies that can result from that.

At the base monthly wage they are making, it would take nearly two months for one of these workers to afford the Thomas the Train mountain set that sells for $400, made in China.

We have seen this story repeated over and over again, American companies moving production to China to take advantage of cheap labor, poor labor enforcement, and then resell these goods back to the United States. This business model is pursued by hundreds and hundreds of American companies—think about this. A company shuts down in Steubenville or Toledo, Ohio, moves its production to Wuhan or Beijing, gets tax breaks doing it and then sells those products back into the home country.

It is not good for the environment. It is not good for communities and you can see what it does. For all intents and purposes, it is a business model for all we can see, unprecedented in human history. Shut down production in one country, move it overseas, sell the production back into the original country.

Eight years ago I introduced the Decent Working Conditions and Fair Competition Act to expand the Tariff Act of 1930 to prohibit the importation of goods made with sweatshop labor. Private industry said we don't need a law. Members could deal with the problem on their own through codes of conduct, through certifications, through audits.

Eight years later, the problem has not gone away. What I want to know today is are corporate codes and self-policing sufficient or do we need a new approach? Does the toy industry in China need something like the legally binding Bangladesh Accord, which I urged companies like Walmart and Target to join last year or an anti-sweatshop law like the one I introduced eight years ago?

We need to do something. We need to be able to tell our children that the person who made their toys, perhaps the mother or the father of a child like them, just living in another country, worked in a good place where she made a decent living. We cannot say that now.

I look forward to hearing from the witnesses. I will begin the introductions and then look forward to the testimony of the four of you.

Kevin Slayton is the interpreter. I happened to go to the school opening of his middle school before he was old enough to be in middle school, many years ago. He is the interpreter. I think you lived in Taiwan for a while, you have studied at Ohio State and learned to speak Mandarin very, very well there.

I will introduce the four principals. Li Qiang is the founder and executive director of China Labor Watch. He has 20 years of experience in labor rights. He has led hundreds of investigations into labor conditions at factories in China, including 100 toy factories. He has written opinion pieces and given numerous media interviews on working conditions. He testified before this Commission two years ago. Welcome, Li Qiang.

William Reese is the president and CEO of the International Youth Foundation, which he has served since 1998. He is a non-industry member of the Governance Board of the ICTI CARE Foundation, established by the International Council of Toy Industries [ICTI] in 2002 to promote fair labor standards and safe working conditions in the production of toys through an auditing and certification system. He serves as a board member for Worldwide Responsible Accredited Production [W.R.A.P.] which certifies the apparel industry. Welcome, Mr. Reese.

Earl Brown is a labor and employment law counsel and China program director for the Solidarity Center at the AFL–CIO. Mr. Brown has represented trade unions and employees in U.S. labor and civil rights litigation for coming up on 40 years, 30-some many years. He was previously general counsel for the Teamsters. He testified before the Commission in 2012 on worker rights. Welcome, Mr. Brown.

Brian Campbell is the director of policy and legal programs at the International Labor Rights Forum [ILRF]. He is responsible for policy, legal, and legislative advocacy for efforts to end child labor and forced labor. For a decade, he has directed ILRF China programs where he has partnered with local organizations to develop a program to train legal advocates, including judges, arbitrators, mediators, and attorneys to promote rule of law through improving enforcement of workers' legal rights in China. Mr. Campbell, welcome to you.

Li Qiang, if you would begin.

STATEMENT OF LI QIANG, EXECUTIVE DIRECTOR AND FOUNDER, CHINA LABOR WATCH [CLW]

Mr. QIANG [interpreted by Kevin Slaten]. I want to thank the Commission for organizing this hearing. I come here not only as an activist, but I also come as a father of two children.

Liu Pan, who began working at the Yiuwah Factory at the age of 15, got his arm stuck in a machine before his entire body was pulled in. His head was crushed beyond recognition when his family saw him. Liu was only 17 when he died.

The factory where he worked had passed Disney's audit and was making Disney products during the time of Liu Pan's death. After media reports, Disney said it would improve conditions, but in the end, it removed its orders from the Yiuwah plant.

This is his ID when he went in the factory. He was a young person. Tragedies like this are the result of poor labor conditions.

CLW's recent investigation of four toy factories discovered serious labor abuses that included a hiring discrimination against minority groups, detaining of workers personal IDs, safety hazards like uninspected machines and locked safety exits, a lack of safety training, insufficient purchase of social insurance as required by law, mandatory excessive overtime, unpaid wages, abuse of management, ineffective audits, and more.

These types of abuses represent a lack of improvement in the toy manufacturing industry's labor conditions over the previous few years. For instance, toy workers in the factories we recently investigated earn one-third less in wages and benefits than Foxconn workers when controlling for working hours.

The primary reason for deteriorating labor conditions in the toy industry is profit. Brand companies suppress the production price at factories and factories, in turn, maintain a profit on the backs of its workers. Toy companies have stringent demands in regard to product materials and quality, so labor costs ultimately become the only flexible input. Workers who are situated at the bottom of this system are forced to bear the costs.

These labor violations are an injustice for workers. They are also a risk for investors and stockholders. For example, we have deduced through our investigation that two of Mattel's directly controlled factories, in just the past year, owe about $7 million to 9,000 workers in unpaid social insurance fees.

Unpaid insurance led to the massive strike in April at the Nike and Adidas factory called Yue Yuen which resulted in production and back-pay costs of $60 million, according to the Wall Street Journal.

Ultimately, if the toy industry wants to truly reform labor conditions and bring them in line with legal and international standards, there are going to be unavoidably higher costs to pay for the toy companies.

Thank you.

Chairman BROWN. Thank you. Mr. Reese, please proceed.

[The prepared statement of Mr. Qiang appears in the appendix.]

STATEMENT OF WILLIAM S. REESE, PRESIDENT AND CEO, INTERNATIONAL YOUTH FOUNDATION; MEMBER, ICTI CARE FOUNDATION GOVERNANCE BOARD

Mr. REESE. Senator, Thank you for accommodating my need to leave early today for a long-scheduled meeting at the World Bank—given my involvement with the International Youth Foundation Worldwide, as a board member of ICTI CARES, I bring some of those experiences to bear—being aware, responsible and ethical in the process of managing its supply chains.

The program was established because ICTI members, national toy associations, along with their retailer and toy brands were committed to having a comprehensive and unified approach to understanding the conditions under which toys are made; were desirous of supporting a process to help raise standards; and eager to have a way of knowing and rewarding manufacturers with demonstrated positive performance.

I am going to ask that my full comments be a part of the record.

Chairman BROWN. Without objection.

Mr. REESE. We believe our programs have met high standards of ethical manufacturing or pushed those standards to be higher. We are one of the very few industry-specific integrated social compliance organizations in the world. We vet and train internationally recognized accredited audit firms that are then chosen randomly to conduct these audits. Finally, we certify the results of the audits by awarding or not awarding a seal of compliance to the factories.

We do this transparently. Our code of business practice, performance standards, audit procedures, seals of compliance, et cetera are all publicly available on our Web site.

Now what we do, the toy firms commit to requiring and accepting ICTI CARE process certification of their suppliers as a way of doing business. We manage the qualification, appointment, and training of highly qualified, internationally accredited audit companies to carry out these audits.

The ICTI CARE Foundation currently uses seven well-trained, well-vetted and accredited audit firms that have undergone a rigorous technical review before we ever start working with them.

A supplier or factory completes an application package to become a member. Once a factory application has been accepted, our operations team in Hong Kong randomly assigns an audit firm from the seven qualified firms that I have mentioned.

Once the audit firm issues a favorable report, the factory will receive a certification seal valid for one year after which it will be subject to another audit, and an unannounced audit. In other words, a factory that comes into the program is audited twice in its first year.

If the audit firm issues a report that identifies any faults, the factory will be required to adopt a corrective action plan and to address those points—point-by-point. Thereafter, a scheduled re-audit is done to ensure that the corrective action plan has been implemented. Factories are put on probation pending correction of identified faults until they are handled.

Now let me talk for a minute about complaint procedures and we are very much interested in taking the proper time and research to reply to CLW and to your Commission. We take allegations seriously. Once we have received a complaint, we jump to action and part of that is in my full report.

Our own audit staff conducts audits, unannounced audits, investigating all of the issues. The process works best when we can work with factories and with NGOs to work through these issues.

However, we don't just investigate and require correction. We also help workers in factories to reach agreement on issues that arise between them.

In closing, Senator, with support of a multi-stakeholder board, which governs the ICTI CARE Board—and we have an annual report here that lists all of the outside non-toy industry people who make up the majority of the board—with a committed operations team in Asia, an experienced and accredited, as I said, social compliance auditors responsible to the brands and retailers supporting the process, we have helped improve the awareness and realization of better working standards in toy factories in China.

We have learned a lot over the past 10 years. We use what we have learned to constantly improve our process and we appreciate this Commission and its seriousness to invite us to testify and we look forward to answering questions and what I cannot answer today in my time, we will certainly answer in writing.

Chairman BROWN. Thank you, Mr. Reese. Thank you for being here. The toy industry was not so cooperative with this hearing. You were—I appreciate that. I am sorry you have to leave early. Jim Yong Kim and what he is doing is very important, but so is this.

Mr. REESE. Thank you. Yes.

Chairman BROWN. Mr. Brown?

[The prepared statement of Mr. Reese appears in the appendix.]

STATEMENT OF EARL V. BROWN, JR., LABOR AND EMPLOYMENT LAW COUNSEL AND CHINA PROGRAM DIRECTOR, SOLIDARITY CENTER, AFL–CIO

Mr. BROWN. Thank you, Senator. I want to first thank you and Chairman Smith and your very able staff for a consistent long-term focus on a very complicated society, China, and for providing a forum for a voice on China. I think it is a major contribution.

I am an American labor lawyer. I work for the human rights and worker rights NGO [non-governmental organization] of the AFL–CIO, the Solidarity Center. Prior to that, I was mainly a courtroom lawyer for trade unions—many unions that are in Ohio for agricultural workers, steelworkers, coal miners—I represented the coal miners for many years.

Since 1999, I have had a privilege of a window on the rise of industrial workers in China and with that rise, the rise of worker voice and worker rights advocacy at the grassroots in China.

I think that industrial workers are key to robust civil society. They are key to deepening space in society and that autonomous worker voice in formal and informal organizations is also an indispensable element of legal compliance. I am not talking about social progress, I am talking about sheer compliance with applicable Chinese and other countries' labor laws.

Without workers at the grassroots, you cannot enforce complicated occupational health and safety regulations and you cannot even—in environments like China—enforce pay laws. It takes workers, and we think and I agree and Li Qiang has found that auditing, social auditing, is like staging Shakespeare's play, "Hamlet," without the Prince of Denmark.

It does not include this complicated element of worker voice, particularly in a society where public reporting, regulatory norms are vague, not precise and there is no testing record of public documentation for compliance with laws. Imagine trying to find out, for example, whether a certain factory in China produces, via prison labor, coffee mugs for importation in the United States.

There are millions of coffee mugs imported into the United States, probably every coffee mug that you drink out of, and the majority are from China.

Chairman BROWN. There is a small startup plant in eastern Ohio.

Mr. BROWN. Well good.

Chairman BROWN. A former pottery center that makes mugs. So you stand corrected, but only a few. Thank you.

Mr. BROWN. Is it a unionized plant?

Chairman BROWN. It has 10 people so far. They are hiring excons there. It is an incredible thing. They have got a big thing—never mind. Go ahead Mr. Brown.

Mr. BROWN. Okay.

[Laughter.]

Chairman BROWN. I hope that it is, but it is not yet.

Mr. BROWN. Well we hope that they will have worker voice in the United States as well.

So imagine trying to find out that this state-involved enterprise—who owns it, who is profiting, who the agents are in the chain that ship the coffee mugs to the United States, who orders them, what the brands do? Imagine trying to find that out in China. People are afraid even to go to local government offices and ask for documents because their identity will be reported.

Industrial workers, as I mentioned, I think are key to robust civil society. They are also very complicated and the audit model is translating a financial model to a social situation. You cannot find out in China or anywhere else, really, whether occupational health and safety is a reality on the shop floor or way down underground unless you talk to workers. To talk to workers and get them to talk to you, you have to develop trust.

This social investigation is the missing element of social auditing. I think if we are looking to what the U.S. Government should do—remove from the geopolitics, it should fund and support to a greater degree than it does and bring to the table the grassroots networks of workers in China and the worker rights advocates like Li Qiang.

Chairman BROWN. Thank you, Mr. Brown.

Mr. Campbell?

[The prepared statement of Mr. Brown appears in the appendix.]

STATEMENT OF BRIAN CAMPBELL, DIRECTOR OF POLICY AND LEGAL PROGRAMS, INTERNATIONAL LABOR RIGHTS FORUM

Mr. CAMPBELL. Thank you, Mr. Chairman, for inviting me to share some ideas for tools that the U.S. Government can employ that will bring an end to the terrible abuses facing factory workers in China and in other countries.

As was well-documented in China Labor Watch's report and testimony, the sweatshops are the result of complex modern business practices by multi-national enterprises. The reasons sweatshops exist are not complicated. Sweatshops are the result of high-stakes, intense cost and production pressures placed on local companies in China by multi-national enterprises.

Unfortunately during peak production season, the demands of the buyer can lead directly to coercive management policies and in many cases force labor to meet production demands. For example, in the case of Mattel Electronics Dongguan and Zhongshan Coronet factories, China Labor Watch documented in their report how workers who initially voluntarily came to work for the company eventually found themselves unable to leave during the peak season without having to leave behind wages that were already legally owed to them.

With such dire consequences for workers, it is vital that the Chinese and United States Governments work closely together using all of the tools at their disposal to bring an end to the root causes of these labor abuses. In doing so, it is important that we remember two immutable facts that most inform any course of action.

First, unless workers can access a legally binding remedy, they stand to lose if they raise complaints, use grievance processes or take other actions to protect their rights. As is clearly demonstrated in China Labor Watch's reports, workers are the most vulnerable person in the supply chain. They are simultaneously unable to protect themselves from management retaliation and from the economic hit caused by loss of business when companies use CSR [corporate social responsibility] policies incorporated into supplier contracts to rescind the contracts.

Second, global multi-national enterprises and the companies that comprise them like Mattel and Fisher-Price exist by virtue of a grant of authority from governments and legislatures like our Congress which endow them with one overarching legal duty that defines the very nature of this corporate person's character, a fiduciary duty to maximize profits on behalf of shareholders. As a result, business practices employed by companies like Mattel, such as lean production time CSR programs are designed to achieve this singular duty, to protect shareholder interests, though there may be other ancillary benefits from time to time.

In order to strike a new balance between the myopic profit-maximizing nature of the corporate person and human beings impacted by their business practices, the United States and Chinese Governments have already taken an important step by endorsing the UN Guiding Principles on Business and Human Rights.

In line with the OECD [Organisation of Economic Co-operation and Development] guidelines for multi-national enterprises, another international agreement, the Guiding Principles provide a mutual framework for addressing human rights violations and global supply chains that cross national borders. It is based on three fundamental principles.

First, governments have a duty to protect human rights. Second, multi-national enterprises have a responsibility to respect human rights. Third, victims such as exploited migrant workers have a right to a meaningful, effective remedy from both governments and the companies.

However, in order to implement the respect, protect and remedy framework, Congress must pass the necessary laws, including amending already existing legislation to reflect these principles and to ensure that effective remedies are in place for victims. Every agency of the government has to take on their share of this work.

First, Congress must ensure that companies cannot import goods made with forced labor. This would require amending the Tariff Act of 1930.

Second, Congress should pass H.R. 4842 and the Senate should have a companion bill, which is the Business and Supply Chain Transparency Act. This is a vital first step toward ensuring that multi-national enterprises implement their duty to respect or do no harm because it legally mandates reporting on their due diligence requirements. But we need to go further.

Third, as a government consumer, we must act to put in protections for our government supply chain. These must go beyond just forced labor, but tackle the root causes of forced labor like these sweatshop conditions.

Fourth, Congress should help the United States provide dispute resolution through the OECD national contact point. That means providing them the mandate and the resources.

Finally, I applaud President Obama for announcing that they will implement a National Action Plan for implementing these UN Guiding Principles and I call on Congress to support that effort and to pass the laws necessary to do so. Thank you very much.

[The prepared statement of Mr. Campbell appears in the appendix.]

Chairman BROWN. Mr. Campbell, thank you.

Let me start with Mr. Reese since you have to leave. Mr. Brown said that basically auditing falls short. You don't talk to workers enough, all of the criticisms he made. Tell me why he is wrong.

Mr. REESE. Well, social auditing won't solve all issues, but social auditing and even the auditing we do in our own country here is a snapshot in time and when it shows that there are issues that need to be worked on, then you fix them and work on them. And that is what our social auditing is all about.

It takes into account worker voices because there is a helpline in which workers—and we have copies, actually, of a card that each of them carries around with them and is issued and trained to use where there is a helpline that a worker can call in and say here is a problem I am having on the job and those issues are dealt with. So there is a voice.

Chairman BROWN. Do you have the feeling that a worker in one of these plants—Li Qiang talked about the 17-year-old who is young and from a small town and probably a little scared coming to the big city or coming to this plant and has never really seen anything like this in his life—you think they are going to believe calling some place is confidential?

Mr. REESE. First of all, we talk to and train the workers so that they can believe in that. And then I think we only earn our credibility because we follow up on their calls.

Chairman BROWN. And any of these others, feel free to speak because I want this to be more of a conversation, but I am sort of starting with Mr. Reese.

Mr. QIANG. During our investigation, the investigator actually called the helpline multiple times in different factories and there was really no effect.

This is a Mattel worker who was beat up by the security guards at the factory. After he was beat up on the grounds, this is what he looked like.

A relative of this worker died at the factory, had committed suicide. They went to protest at the gates and then were beat up by security. After the suicide, they had called the ICTI hotline about this suicide and what the factory did to contribute to it and there was no effect.

The reason this person committed suicide is because she was a 45-year-old female worker who was on the production line and working too slowly for the management's preferences and she was yelled at then, berated, they told her she was working too slow, she could lose her job. She ended up crying on the line because of that pressure, went up to the fourth floor, jumped off and killed herself.

The family demanded 250,000 RMB from the factory, which is roughly $40,000, I think. Up to this point—this is three years ago—they have never received all of that compensation.

Chairman BROWN. Thank you, Li Qiang.

Mr. Reese, we delayed this hearing a little while because you needed more time to investigate the allegations raised in the China Labor Watch report. Share some of the findings that you have.

Mr. REESE. Okay, Senator, we received the report on November 18, when you received it. Our operations people are looking into all of those issues right now and we will get back to you, but we do not—it has only been a few weeks ago and there are a lot of issues and we will look into every one of them and publish our summary report and make sure you get a copy.

Chairman BROWN. This report will be totally public?

Mr. REESE. Yes.

Chairman BROWN. You publish?

Mr. REESE. Yes.

Chairman BROWN. Okay.

Mr. REESE. All of our summary reports are put up on our Web site.

[The report appears in the appendix.]

Chairman BROWN. Do you disclose information about plants that have lost their certification and do you explain—or been put on probation—including specific reasons? Do you publish that? Do you make that public so that people know that?

Mr. REESE. We publish—and I will have to ask maybe a colleague of mine here to put—to either add or put it back in writing to you, but we certainly publish which firms are accredited and are no longer accredited or put on probation.

Chairman BROWN. And do you explain why those companies, those firms were put on probation or were decertified?

Mr. REESE. Our audits show that, yes. Yes, our audits show that.

Chairman BROWN. And they show not just the fact that they were decertified or on probation but——

Mr. REESE. Our audits are specific with factories as to why they were decertified, yes.

Chairman BROWN. I understand that toy companies commit to buy from only certified factories, but that this is voluntary. Is that correct?

Mr. REESE. Well, it is not viewed as voluntary by the factories of American firms who commit to it. Yes, it—the Commitment—is voluntary to the American firms. They have signed the ICTI CARE Process pledge to commit to buying their things from——

Chairman BROWN. So all of these major companies that we have heard of Mattel and Hasbro, they only buy in China from companies that are certified?

Mr. REESE. That is right.

Chairman BROWN. And that is what your experience is Mr. Campbell and Mr. Brown?

Mr. BROWN. My experience is that—in preparation for this hearing, I went back over a list of reports about the toy industry since 1999, they all read the same. There is a 1999 report that reads like Li Qiang's report, that these organizations of the United States and the people down the chain do not even know, sometimes, who the contracting is going to.

So this idea that a certification program is effective in controlling the supply chain, I think belies the complexity and the lack of disclosure in supply chains.

Chairman BROWN. Mr. Reese, that begs the question—you certified a factory. That factory's behavior is acceptable. That factory then subcontracts to another factory that is not certified. How do you stop that from happening?

Mr. REESE. That is a very complex issue and I must say we are working on that. Right now we are certifying the factory.

Chairman BROWN. You certify the first factory, but that factory might buy from a factory that is not certified in a lot of those practices.

Mr. REESE. That is right.

Chairman BROWN. So does that not concern you?

Mr. REESE. We are trying to push that out through the supply chains, but that is—you are absolutely right, Earl. It is a very complex situation and it does not lend itself easily to quick checklists. But our continuous improvement program is absolutely about getting the supply chains to push that out.

Chairman BROWN. I remember when we did hearings. Senator Kennedy asked me to do some hearings on the HELP [Health, Education, Labor, and Pensions] Committee years ago on the supply chain in pharmaceuticals. Pfizer and a number of other companies were not even able to trace where all of their ingredients came from because there was such a long "fingery"—if you will—supply chain which begs the question that shouldn't they be responsible for the safety of their drugs regardless of—the FDA cannot go to China and regulate every village where some ingredients, where the first component comes from.

So what are you doing about that? You have had a number of years with this voluntary certification. What progress have you made reaching further out in the supply chain where you have—there are the safety issues that are pronounced there, but there is the purpose of this hearing and frankly the most important purpose, I think, is the safety of these workers.

How are you reaching them? What progress have you made in these years?

Mr. REESE. Well, you are absolutely right, our goal is to improve the working conditions for the workers themselves and that is their hours, that is their pay, that is making sure that they are of age, their health systems, their safety systems and those issues and that is exactly what the Code of Conduct audits. And it helps companies that are not reaching it to become properly certified or they are terminated.

Mr. BROWN. Senator?

Chairman BROWN. Yes, Mr. Brown?

Mr. BROWN. I want to address a little bit the complexity argument. Complexity points to the need for a system of garnering worker input which workers can trust and is shielded from the power of the employer to punish people for telling the truth.

Labor rights networks and labor rights advocates, given the legal structure of China, are one key element of that and I do not believe a bunch of auditors and a bunch of managers and a bunch of memos going down through corporations and their suppliers can grasp the facts of labor law compliance on the factory floor.

Chairman BROWN. So, Mr. Reese is saying that this compliance—the auditors can make these plants safer with the work they do. You think it has to be more or in addition empowering workers to be able to point those out and you are saying Mr. Reese's construct of voluntary audits and certification cannot really bring those workers' voices in as thoroughly as they need to be?

Mr. BROWN. Exactly. I used to represent coal miners' mine safety committees. And I learned one thing. You can have engineers and everybody else, but it is the worker at the plant who knows whether he is getting paid right or she knows whether she is getting paid right, who knows that this load is too heavy or this pace is too fast, not a 25-year-old accountant from one of the four accounting firms that somehow are able to pretend that they don't interweave in a way that presents some conflict of interest. But I will leave that to another thing—can do.

Chairman BROWN. Li Qiang, what have you found in your studies?

Mr. QIANG. This auditing system is really of no use. It is really directed at investors. It is to lower risks so investors look at these reports and sort of calculate whether or not there is a risk in the supply chain.

They do it once or twice a year when they come, the factories prepare for it. They can adapt and pass it that way.

The factories that we have investigated, not just these ones, but in the past as well, they have all been audited multiple times, not just by ICTI, but also by companies—their own auditors.

Chairman BROWN. Mr. Campbell, did you want to comment on that?

Mr. CAMPBELL. Thank you very much. Yes, I want to comment just generally on the overall concept and just build a little bit on something that Li Qiang said which is, the primary duty of the company that I mentioned in my testimony is profit maximization. And so the audit systems, in my experience, have really been designed as a defensive tool. It is to protect the reputation of the company. And there is a value to that.

There is a value to a company's reputation for workers and I want to actually say that, too, because there are workers who are committed to companies. There are workers who have been working at companies for many years. When they lose their sales, those workers suffer and that is something important to remember, too.

It is not to say that there is not anything that we can do, but it is to say that there are conflicting interests that are inherently involved in this economic relationship. I think what is important here is that—let me give you an example. Several years ago, my organization and Terry Collingsworth, a tremendous attorney, brought a suit that I was able to work on, against Walmart.

We came across workers and supply chains that were not getting paid overtime, forced overtime, all of the problems. Representing these workers—and they were from many different countries—we filed a lawsuit on their behalf, on the behalf of Chinese workers in U.S. court because Walmart incorporated this code of conduct in their contract.

Contract law in California says that if you incorporate a contract clause to benefit a third party, that third party is a party to the contract and therefore, can take specific action to enforce that contract. In this case, we lost and the workers lost the case because Walmart had to admit in court that they never intended to benefit the workers with their code of conduct.

It was intended as a defensive tool. And so therefore, the court in the 9th Circuit had to rule. They said, "Well, as a result, there was no intent to benefit the worker. So, therefore, we cannot say that this is for the worker. So, therefore, they are not a party."

So when you hear companies talk about incorporating codes into their contracts and stuff, they are not legally binding just because they are in a contract. And that is important. Workers need legally binding remedies.

If they call a complaint process, they cannot rely on the company to provide money. They need an independent process, arbitration, mediation. These types of processes will guarantee that workers have access to justice.

These are not offered by social auditing. I think social auditing— I think it is important companies understand due diligence is important. It plays a role. But again, it is not going to solve the problem.

What we need are remedies, legal remedies that companies commit to. And I think the Bangladesh Accord is a good example of one, where there is a legally binding remedy if the factory is

14

found—in Bangladesh—to not be in compliance, than the companies have agreed to an arbitration that is enforceable in the home country of that company and that arbitration is to secure the funds from that company who promised by contract, which is by law now, to provide the money to help fix that factory.

It could go further and this is what we need in the toy industry. We do not have a problem with factory structures. We have a problem with forced overtime and peak production seasons and lean production.

So I think it is really important that we focus on what the problems are and come up with some legally binding remedies that companies are willing to legally commit to, enforceable in courts that will allow for workers to raise grievances and feel they can do so in a protected way. Thank you.

Chairman BROWN. Sure. Mr. Reese, what does ICTI CARE think about the Bangladesh Accord, what he was talking about?

Mr. REESE. Frankly, that is another industry in another country. Our work is predominately in China with the toy industries and most of the Bangladesh work, which I do know about from another association because I serve on the W.R.A.P. Board, that is about mostly apparel and it is about Bangladesh and fire and all of those things.

Now there are safety issues that are a part of our audit. I must say whether an auditor is 25, 35, or 45, they are well-trained in what they are doing. They are audited by us as to assure how good their auditing is. They are trained in the code. They are trained in social auditing.

Auditing is a snapshot. Auditing is not the entire solution to changing these things, but it gives you the snapshot of what needs to be improved and our program is about improving the working conditions of workers.

Chairman BROWN. What else have you advocated? If you say auditing is a snapshot and auditing is helpful, but it is not a full solution, what is your organization recommending beyond the auditing?

Mr. REESE. There are surprise audits and secondary audits when we have some disputes. Ultimately, too, some of this is about the governance of China and how they manage their own laws.

We, personally, are not a lobbying outfit. We are not pushing public policy. Personally, though, I would like to see workers able to organize and protest or express their rights, but that is not our role. We are there to improve the working conditions of workers through the social auditing and compliance of these supply chains.

We give workers a voice. Now I must tell you. And we will look into calls that were not answered or calls where there is some evidence about what happened. But what we have found is that the majority of the calls are about the quality of food or their dormitory or something like this.

A lot of calls are actually by workers who want to work more hours. But there are calls, too, that come in from workers who say I am being forced to work overtime or I am working overtime and not getting paid. Well, that triggers an immediate second audit by us and can terminate the certification if that is proven.

Chairman BROWN. Li Qiang, do you want to speak and then I have a question.

Mr. QIANG. Yes, workers do want more overtime. That is because their base wage is too low. Without doing a tremendous amount of overtime, they do not have a living wage. How are you going to raise a family on a couple hundred dollars in a place where prices are going up? Raise a family—you have kids, you have a spouse. You cannot live on these wages.

And the factory uses this against workers as a punishment. If workers are not listening to what the management wants, if they are pushing back against management, management will say I just won't give you any overtime and they know that that means they will not have a living wage.

In the toy industry there is a seasonal nature. In the busy season the factories will make workers take on a tremendous amount of overtime and sort of some of the conditions that we saw here.

In the off season, the factory wants the workers to quit, but if they fire them, they have to pay them compensation according to law. So they take away all of their overtime intentionally, restrict a lot of workers from having any overtime and the workers have no choice but to leave because it is not a living wage. And when they quit, they do not get compensation because under Chinese law, you do not have to give them compensation.

Chairman BROWN. You do not have to give them compensation for the hours that they have already worked?

Mr. QIANG. No. I am sorry. Severance pay.

Chairman BROWN. Severance pay.

Mr. QIANG. As well as social insurance that has not been paid. We see this very commonly in China. There has been social insurance that has not been paid that is required by law over months and workers have no chance of getting any of that back pay if they quit.

Chairman BROWN. Mr. Reese said that part of this is the problem with Chinese law or the enforcement of Chinese law, not surprising. The UN Guiding Principles on Business and Human Rights—mentioned by Mr. Campbell—the Chinese have endorsed it. What are your thoughts about China doing more than saying they are for these principles, getting them enforced in the higher echelons of Chinese society or Chinese Government to begin to enforce these principles? Answer that and then I want to follow up.

Mr. REESE. Senator, could I jump in? I apologize for having to leave. I have stayed 15 minutes longer than I was supposed to, but we will get back to you on all questions that have been raised up until now and after this in writing to both you and the Commission as may be requested.

Chairman BROWN. Thank you, Mr. Reese. Do you want to answer that first? He is explaining that.

Mr. BROWN. I just wanted to say that food in militarized factories where people are congregated in dormitories, that live in dormitories and their sole source in some of these areas for food is the factory is a vital issue. Very similar, it does not rank below pay and if you are a factory worker and you have to carry water up 8 flights after a 12-hour shift, that is also a very concrete issue.

And worker voice comes out in all these various things. So the complexity argument argues for incorporation of organizations that

Mr. Li Qiang works with into the process of determining whether there is compliance.

Chairman BROWN. Okay.

Mr. QIANG. This problem with law enforcement in China actually has two aspects to it. There is the government aspect, there is also the company aspect because the companies have to respect the law and the government has to enforce it.

The way it works in China, usually, is that the companies will go sort of lobby local government and tell them we want to surpass working hour laws. We do not want to pay all of the social insurance that is required by law. And they get this sort of permission from the local government to do so.

So for example with working hours, you might know that Chinese labor law does not permit more than 36 hours of overtime a month. A lot of factories, many factories will go to the local government and ask them for permission to surpass this 36-hour law and they will often get it. They will just get this permission and it allows them to do—there is no real limit according to the written permission they have. They get this permission from the local government to do so.

Chairman BROWN. A number of those companies that you say— for want of a better term—lobby local Chinese officials, I assume a number of those companies are either U.S. companies, Western companies or contracting with Western companies; correct?

Mr. QIANG. Yes.

Chairman BROWN. Li Qiang, do you see any difference between European companies' behavior in China to weaken standards for workers—pay, bathroom breaks, food in the dormitories, a whole host of issues, safety? Do you see American companies much different from European companies or Japanese companies in China? Is their behavior pretty similar?

Mr. QIANG. It is very similar. For example, two of the factories— we were just talking about this report. Two of the factories we looked at were directly managed and owned by Mattel.

Maybe 10 years ago there was a difference. The foreign-owned companies like the Mattel factories were found or even if they are European-owned, they might have been much better than the local contractors, but nowadays, they are very similar, sort of a similar level now.

Chairman BROWN. This is, in some cases, American companies or German companies or companies contracting with them, they will go—but clearly subcontracting with Mattel or Hasbro or a European company that will go directly to local Chinese officials to weaken some of the provisions of Chinese law that protect workers?

Mr. QIANG. Yes, that is right. So in the case—for example, again of these Mattel factories, both of these factories we recorded during our investigation had excessive overtime.

In order to do that in a sort of so-called legal way, they would have had to have gone to the local government to get this permission.

Chairman BROWN. So if instead of—we asked, I believe, Hasbro and Mattel to be here, they declined. If they had joined us—if the CEO of Mattel or Hasbro were sitting there right now and you said what you said, what would you say now—what would he say?

Mr. QIANG. They would say they are a part of the ICTI process. And they would say it is an industry issue.

Chairman BROWN. Would they deny having gone to local officials to weaken the laws, to weaken the enforcement?

Mr. QIANG. They are even more clear about what is going on in the factories than we are. I have met with Hasbro and Mattel executives and they very well understand what is going on in these factories.

I remember meeting with somebody from Mattel when I was in Hong Kong and they directly told me we have permission from the government to have these sort of overtime hours. So they were defending themselves with that——

Chairman BROWN. So they acknowledge going to the local governments and getting this permission on overtime and back pay and some of these things and not paying social insurance and——

Mr. QIANG. I did not bring that up directly when I was in that meeting, but with overtime, yes. They admitted getting this permission from the government, going to the government to get their permission.

Chairman BROWN. Thank you. Mr. Campbell, if the Congress passed a Decent Working Conditions and Fair Competition Act, prohibit importation of goods made with sweatshop labor and empower the FTC [Federal Trade Commission] and all of the things that went with it, what would happen?

Mr. CAMPBELL. I think what would happen right out of the gate is that the industry is going to take these issues much more seriously. Currently, U.S. law prohibits the importation of goods made with forced labor and there are a few things that need to change in that law for it to actually function.

As the report documented very well, there is a very fine, thin line between poor working conditions, sweatshop conditions that then at peak production times turn into brief periods of forced labor. Forced labor is not just slavery.

I think looking at how that law has functioned, I think what is important is to recognize that, first, there needs to be a remedy because, again, when you do detain a product, it is going to send economic financial ramifications back down the supply chain and we do not want to hurt the victims. The victims here are, remember, these forced-labor workers in China.

So we need to figure out how to work better with the Chinese Government to ensure that remedies are available when action is taken. But action still should be taken because no one should be profiting from what are, on the forced-labor side, crimes and other violations of what are local laws.

I think it needs to be done in a coordinated way and it needs to be surgical. It cannot just be like an entire industry. It needs to be the Mattel factory. We have the information, we have the investigation and we know where the products are coming into if that is one of the factories that is under investigation.

So I think expanding it to sweatshops would actually be the way to achieve the ultimate goal of the forced labor because that is where it starts. And so I think it is a good idea. I think trade, though, can be a difficult issue because of the challenge on the remedy side.

Often, I think, if you just detain the product, companies will just cut ties with those factories. So when examining legislation like this, I would make sure that there is some way to ensure that the victims get financial remedies and others that they need to make themselves whole.

And that could be done in many different ways. I know that victims of forced labor who are currently being—that there are currently cases. The Department of Justice prosecutes under U.S. law. There are funds available to them. They are not yet available when dealing with these issues overseas because of the way investigations work.

But I think all of that can be fixed and I think it can be a workable idea as long as it is surgical and there is good cooperation on all sides.

Chairman BROWN. Li Qiang, are things getting worse in the toy industry?

Mr. QIANG. Relative to the past, it is getting worse. If you look at other factories that have really gotten a lot of attention before, like Foxconn as a sweatshop, for example, Foxconn's conditions have improved a little bit even if it still has problems. For example, I mentioned in my testimony that wages of Foxconn workers are now one-third higher than these toy factory workers if you control for hours they work.

Just to emphasize that point, if the same worker was in a toy factory, the Foxconn factory, and they did the exact same amount of working hours in the same region, in the same area, the toy worker would make one-third less.

Chairman BROWN. Speaking of that, Mr. Brown, and this probably is my last question. Are the problems you described equally applicable to toys as to the electronics industry? Do you see pretty significant similarities across the board, Mr. Li Qiang's comment notwithstanding?

Mr. BROWN. I think his report and all of the 20 years of auditing of the toy industry and other industries show a systemic similarity. It is all the same.

If I could just return to the point of local government, the subcontractors in this chain, the principal prime subcontractors are all colluding with local government to avoid Chinese labor law. For example, to pay the statutorily required social insurance contributions, they get a little chit from the local government lowering it and it is a major cause of industrial strife and it is a major labor abuse.

Chairman BROWN. Would Mattel and Hasbro argue that those local governments are democratically selected?

Mr. BROWN. No, they would not. And I think that helps the penetration——

Chairman BROWN. I understand that they are not, but would they argue they are? Would they sit here and argue——

Mr. BROWN. I have never heard anyone argue that.

Chairman BROWN. Well, I understand that. They also are not here and they did not want to testify. So if they are justifying going to a government agency that is supposed to represent the public to get lower wages, temporarily during the season Mr. Campbell talks about, the busy season, toy manufacture season, the fall, late sum-

19

mer, fall, whenever it is, would they argue that those local governments are actually representing the Chinese people? Never heard them do that?

Mr. BROWN. I have never heard them do that and I am trying to puzzle how they could.

Chairman BROWN. Mr. Li Qiang, go ahead.

Mr. QIANG. As you may know, the situation in China, with the majority of workers in these factories being migrant workers, internal migrant workers, they come from other provinces. So a lot of these workers are going to Guangdong, for example, where the majority of manufacturing takes place for the toy industry.

The local government does not see these migrants as their constituency, so to speak. In the end, they are going to go home or they figure they are going to go home. They are not responsible for their welfare after they leave. They are not responsible for their retirement. They are not responsible for the benefits. Their household registration is not in that region. So this really makes the local government more like a business because it doesn't really see these people as constituents.

Chairman BROWN. Li Qiang, you mentioned Foxconn, you both mentioned Foxconn, that pay is maybe one-third higher. Is that entirely because of public pressure in this country and the embarrassment of Apple and some of these major American iconic companies that——

Mr. QIANG. I do think it's because of public pressure. Starting in 2010 and 2011 when Foxconn really appeared in the news and a lot of organizations were reporting on them. And some of these improvements have also brought along the entire industry. So you will see some of these similar improvements in other electronics factories.

Chairman BROWN. Why have we not been successful at shining a light on Mattel and Hasbro and the big American toymakers in the same way?

Mr. QIANG. It is really a lack of attention. Generally speaking, there has been so much attention on the electronics industry. If you look from 2007–2008 when maybe the toy industry was a little more on top on things, they were more willing to change things, ever since then the electronics industry has gotten so much attention in the media and the attention, relatively speaking, toward the toy industry has gone down. So this has brought the same sort of relevant decline in working conditions.

For example just with this recent report—well, if you were to publish the Foxconn report or even electronics report, you will get reports from the AP, the Wall Street Journal, the New York Times, all of the big news companies will report on it. But this last report that we did with the toy company, there is very little reporting in the media. There is just not as much attention on toy issues.

So the toy industry is taking advantage of the fact that they have less attention, to be less enthusiastic or active about these reforms and you see the relative decline in the labor conditions as a result.

Chairman BROWN. Mr. Brown, last words?

Mr. BROWN. Very last words. I think there should be more standing for public interests advocates to intervene and propose rem-

20

edies in trade disputes like the sweatshop law that Mr. Campbell discussed. I think that is very important.

Chairman BROWN. I thank you all for joining us. This will conclude the hearing.

Congressman Smith has a statement that we will enter into the record.

[The prepared statement of Representative Smith appears in the appendix.]

Chairman BROWN. Any additional comments you want to make, we would love to have for the record. We may send letters to each of you asking for more comments, if you would please within a week turn those letters around and give us answers.

I appreciate the advocacy of all of you for those that clearly need a voice in this world.

The Commission is adjourned.

[Whereupon, at 11:54 a.m., the hearing was concluded.]

APPENDIX

PREPARED STATEMENTS

PREPARED STATEMENT OF LI QIANG

DECEMBER 11, 2014

FAIR TOYS FOR OUR KIDS

I am the founder and Executive Director of the New York-based China Labor Watch (CLW) and a labor activist that has participated in China's labor rights movement for over twenty years, including investigation of toy factories that began in 1999. To date, I have led research on labor conditions of more than 100 toy factories. The reason I am testifying before Congress today is not only because for years I have observed the toy industry's poor labor conditions, it is also because I recently became the father of two children and have come to fully understand the importance of improving the conditions and rights of workers in the toy industry as a result.

I care deeply about my children's safety and make sure that they do not leave my sight, whether at home or outside. I want for my children to grow up safely, and I also hope that they develop empathy. When I take my son to the toy store, its shelves overflowing with Mickey Mouse, Transformers, Barbie Dolls, and little planes, cars, and balls. His face is always brimming with joy as he stops in front of each toy. Every time I see this, I come under a lot of pressure, because I understand that behind American fairytales made in China, there is often a tragic story, and I do not want my child's happiness to be connected to this.

When I take my son to Toys R Us to look at Disney toys, I often think of a boy named Liu Pan who died at the age of 17 while working at the Yiuwah Factory in Dongguan, China. Liu, who had been working at the factory for two years already, was so exhausted by the conditions of his work that he let his hand and then entire body get trapped in a machine. After Liu's death was publicized in the media, Disney announced that the factory he worked at was responsible for less than 15% of Disney's orders, and since it did not meet Disney's labor standards, Disney pulled out of the factory and would have no further relationship with it.

This kind of heartbreaking story is not limited to Disney. A similar tragedy occurred in a Mattel factory, where a 45-year old mother of two named Hu Nianzhen was reprimanded by her manager in front of her co-workers for working too slowly on the production line. The manager threatened that the company would fire her for slow working speed and forced her to leave the production line, prompting Hu to sob in the workshop. While no one was paying attention, Hu climbed to the fourth floor. Shortly after, a bang was heard throughout the workshop; Hu had thrown herself from the roof and died immediately. Neither the factory nor Mattel accepted any responsibility for her death. When Hu's family sought out the factory for an explanation, they were severely beaten outside the factory's gates by factory guards. They were later forced to sign a compensation agreement which awarded them only 90,000 RMB ($14,580).

These stories are not just outliers; they were caused by the terrible labor conditions within the toy industry.

Between June and November 2014, CLW carried out another in-depth investigation of labor conditions in the toy manufacturing industry, this time targeting four facilities in Guangdong, China: Mattel Electronics Dongguan (MED), Zhongshan Coronet Toys (Coronet), Dongguan Chang'an Mattel Toys 2nd Factory (MCA), and Dongguan Lung Cheong Toys (Lung Cheong). CLW's investigation confirmed that the factories produce for some of the largest toy brand companies in the world: Mattel and Fisher-Price, Disney, Hasbro, and Crayola, including famous toy brands like Barbie, Mickey Mouse, Transformers' Optimus Prime, and Thomas the Tank Engine. According to company information, the factories also produce toys for other major toy companies and retailers like Target, Kid Galaxy, Spinmaster, Kids II, and Tomy IFI.

CLW's 2014 investigation once again uncovered a long list of labor rights violations, most of which existed in toy supplier factories in 2007, suggesting that over the past seven years, the state of labor conditions in the toy manufacturing industry has failed to improve and are instead deteriorating. During peak season, workers commonly work six days a week, eleven hour a day; do not receive adequate healthcare or insurance nor legally mandated safety training; live in small rooms in factory dorms with 10 or more workers; have their IDs illegally confiscated; are made to jump through hoops if they wish to resign; and are not able to receive due wages if they quit.

A CLW investigator entered the aforementioned four toy factories as a worker, laboring alongside other workers under the same conditions. Other CLW investigators also carried out follow-up assessments in October and November 2014. Through direct experience and hundreds of worker interviews, CLW's investigation discovered a set of 20 legal and ethical labor violations, a summary of which is below.

1. Hiring discrimination: Restrictions on the age and ethnic group of applicants were found as well as a refusal to hire applicants with tattoos.

2. Detaining personal IDs: Two factories illegally detain workers' personal IDs during hiring procedures, one factory for 24 hours, the other for five hours.

3. Lack of physical exams: Three factories do not provide any physical exams to workers before or after being hired, meaning that previous conditions are unknown before going on the job, and if a worker contracts an occupational illness, she may not have the necessary evidence to prove that it was related to work at the factory. While one factory provides physical exams, workers are not given their exam results.

4. Lack of legally mandated safety training: Chinese legal regulations require 24 hours of pre-job safety training for manufacturing workers. In three factories, workers receive half to two hours of pre-job training, much of which is unrelated to occupational safety. The fourth factory conducts absolutely no pre-job training.

5. Workers forced to sign training forms despite lack of training: Three factories force workers to sign forms certifying that they participated in health and safety training that they never actually receive.

6. Labor contract violations: Three companies make workers sign incomplete labor contracts while providing very little time to read the contract and rushing workers to sign it. Workers must wait one to two months after signing to receive a copy of their labor contract, which is a violation of China's Labor Contract Law. A fourth factory fails to sign any labor contracts with temp workers or student workers and only signs contracts with formal workers after a multi-month probation period.

7. Underpayment of legally mandated social insurance: All four factories pay workers' social insurance at a rate below legal obligations.

8. Excessive overtime work: All of the factories investigated have workers accumulate at least 100 hours of overtime a month, with one factory's workers laboring over 120 hours of overtime a month, three times in excess the statutory maximum of 36 hours per month.

9. Unpaid wages: Two factories fail to pay workers overtime wages for daily mandatory work meetings before and after their shifts. The other two factories do not pay workers during mandatory training.

10. Frequent rotation between day and night shifts: One plant rotates workers between day and night shifts once a week and another plant once every two weeks. Such frequent shift rotation has been shown to be harmful to workers' health.

11. Lack of protective equipment: All factories investigated failed to provide workers with sufficient protective equipment despite their coming into regular contact with harmful chemicals.

12. Ill-maintained production machinery: Three plants failed to conduct regular safety inspections of production machinery, based on a lack of inspection records.

13. Poor living conditions: The toy factories investigated generally maintain poor living conditions for their workers, including crowded and hot dorms with 8 to 18 people per room, five shower rooms for 180 people, lax dorm management leading to frequent theft, and fire safety concerns.

14. Fire safety concerns: One factory locks emergency exit doors, and fire escape routes are blocked. None of the factories provide sufficient fire prevention training to workers.

15. Environmental pollution: Industrial waste water is discharged into the general sewer system and a failure to separate industrial waste from general waste.

16. Lack of effective grievance channels: Some of the factories investigated have a complaint hotline, but the phone number is out of order or workers are often told by the operator to simply tell their supervisor about the problem.

17. Lack of union representation: The factories have unions, but most were in name only, failing to actually represent worker interests. One factory had a more active union, but it usually led social activities with workers. Moreover, union representatives are not elected by workers and the union chairman is a member of the company's management team.

18. Illegal resignation procedures: Three factories require workers to obtain management approval before resigning, but Chinese law only requires workers to give notice, not apply for resignation.

19. Abusive management: Management is sometimes verbally abusive to workers. For example, a supervisor in one factory told a worker with sick parents that "even if someone dies in your family you'll not be allowed to resign."

20. Auditing fraud: Two companies were found to use deceptive methods during social audits. In one factory, workers are made by management to hide the truth about working conditions. Another factory even creates a special area for inspection that has better conditions than its other production facilities.

These violations suggest that labor conditions have failed to improve in toy industry supplier factories over the past seven years. And relative to other industries, conditions may even be deteriorating. For instance, over the past few years, workers at electronics manufacturer Foxconn have seen an increase in overall compensation and reduction in working hours. Before calculating overtime wages, the average monthly wage of workers in the four toy factories investigated is 1,335 RMB ($218). But even after illegally excessive overtime hours, working at least six days a week in 12-hour shifts, these toy workers earn between 2,500 RMB ($409) and 3,000 RMB ($490) a month. In comparison, a worker at Foxconn in Chengdu, Zhengzhou, or Shenzhen, despite excessive overtime of 80 hours per month, will earn around 3,500 RMB ($573).

WORKER EXPLOITATION IN THE TOY INDUSTRY

Intense business competition and demand for cheap products drives toy companies to suppress manufacturing prices. Toy sellers, especially international brand companies, have largely moved their manufacturing base from their home countries to developing countries in Asia and Latin America to utilize cheap labor. In order to mitigate investment risk, instead of building their own factories in these regions, toy companies often contract their manufacturing to local factories via intermediary supply chain firms. Supplier factories have little choice but to accept the production price put forward by the toy company. Sometimes, in order to receive the business, factories will even reduce the cost further. But toy companies maintain strict demands on material and product quality, so labor costs ultimately become the only flexible factor. Workers, situated at the bottom of this system, are forced to bear the cost.

Multinationals are keen to benefit from this system. While it reduces their investment risk, it also enables them to distance themselves from factories that act in unethical or illegal ways. The multinationals that do not directly employ workers making their products often rely on this fact when blaming factories for poor or illegal labor conditions.

Many toy companies divide their toy orders among dozens or hundreds of factories in order to ensure that their orders in any given factory only consists of a small proportion of that factory's total orders—usually no more than 20 percent. Toy companies will also use this as a basis for avoiding responsibility for poor labor conditions. For example, if CLW uncovers labor rights violations at a Disney supplier factory in China, Disney might respond that it only maintains a small number of orders in the plant and is unable to influence the factory's behavior. Disney will blame the factory or could even blame other clients of the factory. If public pressure is too intense, toy companies will claim that the factory failed to respect their code of conduct and, on this basis, end business with the plant. In this way, toy companies can make a public show of standing up for workers' rights while reducing their own risk and costs to their business. Instead of acting with a true sense of responsibility, most major toy companies will use coping and delay tactics when faced with labor violations.

In addition to maximizing profit via suppliers, some toy companies will directly manage a number of factories in order to guarantee product quality and inventory. But poor and illegal labor conditions are a universal problem in the toy manufacturing industry, and even these directly controlled factories violate workers' rights. Despite this, the companies who manage these factories will push off responsibility for labor violations to others, claiming that it's an industry problem.

China's workers have naturally attempted to protest the aforementioned circumstances; in 2013, workers at the Shenzhen Baode Toy Factory went on strike to demand improvements in the factory's labor conditions and the social insurance owed to them.

Shenzhen Baode Toy Factory is a typical export-oriented manufacturer which mainly makes products for Mattel and Disney. The factory was built in 1989 and has nearly 10,000 workers at peak periods. At the time of the strike over social insurance payments in August 2013, there were 3,000 workers employed at the factory, a number which dropped to 1,000 after the strike.

According to information received from workers, when data was calculated in May 2013, there were 438 workers who had been at the factory for more than five years, 247 workers who had been at the factory for more than 10 years, 158 workers who had been at the factory for more than 15 years, and 48 workers who had been at the factory for more than 20 years. The social insurance issue was divided between cases were the factory paid less than the amount due or simply had not paid at all.

Among the three thousand workers employed by Shenzhen Baode, divided by their time working at the factory, the number of workers who were at the factory for more than five years and were owed social insurance payments totaled 398; those who were at the factory for more than 10 years and were owed social insurance payments totaled 141; those who were at the factory for more than 15 years and were owed social insurance payments totaled 59. This data is based on the number of workers still in the factory in May 2013; when workers who had left the factory before May are also considered, the proportion of workers owed social insurance payments is even higher.

Local social insurance regulations require that a company pays 17.3% of wages as insurance and each individual pays 8.5% of their wages as insurance. Based on these rules, assuming average monthly wages of 2,000 RMB ($324) and annual wages of 24,000 RMB ($3,888) over the past 10 years, the company would owe each worker 4,152 RMB ($672) per year in insurance backpay, or 41,520 RMB ($6,726) for 10 years of unpaid insurance.

Table 1: Social insurance rates in Guangdong Province

Insurance Type		Enterprise	Individual
Retirement Insurance	Enterprise	11%	8%
	Local	3%	
Work Injury Insurance		1%	
Unemployment Insurance		0.5%	
Health Insurance	In-patient	1.75%	
	Out-patient	0.05%	0.50%

Besides the issues of long-term workers who are owed compensation, after the government mandated that all enterprises purchase social insurance for their workers, new workers also found that their various legally mandated insurances were not paid in full by companies. The base monthly wage of Baode's workers combined with overtime pay and other subsidies came out to 3,000 RMB ($486) per month. According to law, social insurance fees should be paid according to that amount, but the company instead paid insurance according to the local minimum wage of 1,808 RMB ($292) per month, which disregards 1,192 RMB ($193) in overtime wages and subsidies. When calculated in this manner, the company evaded 206 RMB ($33) per month, or 2,475 RMB ($401) per year, in insurance fees for each worker.

The attitudes of the brand companies, factory, and government towards the Baode strike were as follows:

(1) Brand Company Reaction: After the Baode workers began striking over the social insurance issue, Baode's main clients, Disney and Mattel, attempted to distance themselves from the factory by quickly pulling out of production at Baode, explaining the move was primarily for business reasons. In reality, Mattel and Disney had worked with the company for ten years at that point and were aware of the situation with respect to Baode failing to purchase social insurance for its workers. Their actions were a typical method employed by multinational companies to shirk responsibility and place the blame entirely on supplying factories.

(2) Factory Reaction: Baode contracted out its existing orders to other factories, thus reducing the production work for its workers, ensuring they could not receive overtime, and in turn forcing workers to subsist on the minimum wage, which is too low to be considered a living wage. Under these circumstances, many workers were forced to quit, which meant that not only did the factory not have to compensate them for social insurance, but also did not have to provide severance pay. Within three months of the strike, the number of workers at Baode dropped from 3,000 to 1,000.

Baode's actions reflect the typical method that Chinese factories use to lay off workers; not only is it legal, it ensures that companies do not have to pay the compensation they would be required to hand out if they formally terminated workers of their positions rather than forcing them out.

(3) Government Reaction: Baode's workers began petitioning the Shenzhen Guanlan Social Insurance and Labor Offices in addition to the local official labor union in April 2014 but never received any response. In July 2013, the workers petitioned the Shenzhen Municipal People's Congress, Municipal Labor Union, Insurance Bureau, and Legislative Affairs Office, but each of the aforementioned institutions passed responsibility to one another other without giving a clear response to the workers.

In summary, the brand companies, factory, and government each employed various methods to deflect responsibility and create legal loopholes, which ultimately lead to severe violations of workers' rights.

CLW's investigation this year discovered that all four factories had legal violations related to unpaid or insufficiently paid social insurance. For instance, Mattel Electronics Dongguan and Chang'An Mattel 2nd Factory are both directly controlled by Mattel Toys and together employ about 9,000 workers. Based on our conservative estimates, to bring these two plants in accordance with relevant Chinese social insurance regulations, Mattel would need to take on another $7 million in costs, which is about half of a percent of Mattel's 2013 profit of $1.17 billion.

China's economic development has not led to real benefits for its workers, the vast majority of whom still struggle both in work and life. China's economic and political elites are the true beneficiaries of China's economic growth, while the workers have only been on the receiving end of exploitation. Western multinationals have invested heavily in China, but that has not brought about the spread of a system of values which includes human rights and democracy. Instead, these companies have benefited from the lack of protection that a labor union would provide Chinese workers and have quietly exploited them. They have used PR tactics to package their publicly stated labor standards without ever truly executing those standards.

We are by no means powerless in the face of these circumstances. First, we can utilize public hearings such as this one to exert pressure on the toy industry and put forth more media reports to ensure that the public takes note of the production process of toys. Through writing letters or contacting executives at toy companies, we can ensure that those who benefit from the toy industry take action to improve working conditions in toy factories.

Furthermore, we can demand that these toy companies begin by making improvements in the four factories on which we have reported rather than look for excuses to simply pull out of the factory.

Finally, the toy companies should, within the next year, make the aforementioned companies comply with Chinese law as well as the labor standards published by the toy companies themselves. Both must be obeyed fully, and there should be no space to make any excuses. To that end, I have three suggestions for the improvement of labor conditions in the toy industry more broadly:

1. Improving the toy manufacturing industry requires that companies' make their production conditions transparent; all toys should be labeled with their specific factory origin. Factories and brands which have been shown to have committed rights' violations should respond seriously to each violation, in addition to providing an in-depth course of action for making reforms instead of putting forth a general response promising investigations.

2. Guangdong Province is currently carrying out labor union reform pilots. International brand corporations should encourage their suppliers to carry out direct union elections, allowing elected representatives to truly represent the demands of workers and engage in collective bargaining with the factories to protect the rights of workers.

3. Factories must establish effective worker hotlines so that workers may convey labor issues through an independent channel that can ultimately aid workers in successfully resolving work-related problems and protecting their rights.

Why must the improvement of labor conditions begin in the toy industry? Because we cannot let our children grow up with this shadow hanging over them. Let's ensure our children do not also have to face the dirty side of the toy industry after they grow up. Let's ensure that the smiles of our children are founded on just and fair working conditions.

PREPARED STATEMENT OF ICTI CARE FOUNDATION, INC.
PRESENTED BY WILLIAM S. REESE

DECEMBER 11, 2014

Good morning Commissioners, staff, ladies and gentlemen. My name is William Reese and I have been a member of the Governance Board of the ICTI CARE Foundation (ICF) since 2007. On behalf of our board, I would like to thank you for the opportunity to discuss the ICTI CARE Process.

As you may know, the ICTI CARE Foundation does not currently have a CEO, although a new CEO has been appointed and will start in February. Given the timing, we felt it was appropriate for a board member to testify. As a board member I have strong knowledge of our mission, policies and programs, but to the extent that you have detailed questions about operating procedures or specific ICTI CARE Process operations as they relate to individual factories, I may have to defer response to such questions.

Turning to the ICTI CARE Foundation: Because we work to ensure ethical treatment of workers in factories which produce products for children, we believe our programs have to meet high standards in ethical manufacturing. We are one of the very few industry-specific, integrated social compliance organizations in the world. We created a Code of Business Practice in 1991 to define ethical treatment of workers, consistent with national labor laws. We then developed the audit protocols and guidance documents that specify performance standards and audit procedures; we vetted and trained internationally-recognized audit firms that are chosen randomly to conduct our audits; and finally we certify the results of the audits, by either awarding or withholding a Seal of Compliance.

We do this transparently. Our Code of Business Practice, performance standards, audit procedures, Seals of Compliance and our responses to NGOs' reports, such as those from China Labor Watch, are all publicly available on our website.

My presentation focuses on three main areas: who we are, what we do and how we operate when we receive complaints about factories registered in our programs.

Who we are: The ICTI CARE Foundation was incorporated in the state of New York as a non-profit industry association in 2004. The Governance Board was established by the International Council of Toy Industries (a coalition of national toy industry associations) in 2005 and we are just completing our 10th year of operation. Our board is a mixed one of current and former toy industry leaders, civil society and NGOs; and we operate independently of the industry.

The program was established because ICTI's members—national toy associations, along with their retailer and toy brand members, were committed to having a comprehensive and unified approach to understanding the conditions under which toys were made, desirous of supporting a process to help raise standards, and eager to have a way of knowing and rewarding manufacturers for demonstrated performance.

Accordingly, we developed the ICTI CARE Process, the worldwide toy industry's ethical manufacturing program, and have been responsible both for its initial funding and for oversight and guidance as it has grown and evolved.

The ICTI CARE (Caring, Aware, Responsible, Ethical) Process is a global social compliance program, dedicated to promoting fair labor treatment, as well as employee health and safety, in the worldwide supply chain of the toy and juvenile products industries. It provides a single, fair, thorough, transparent and consistent program to monitor factory compliance with ICTI's Code of Business Practices. The Code was promulgated in May 1991 and it has been strengthened and updated periodically, most recently in 2010.

The operations arm of the ICTI CARE Process is the ICTI CARE Foundation Asia, Ltd., located in Hong Kong.

What we do: The main components of the ICTI CARE Process include:

• A program under which toy and children's product marketers, retailers and licensors commit to requiring and/or accepting ICTI CARE Process Certification of their suppliers as meeting the high standards required by the ICTI Code of Business Practice.

• The qualification, appointment and training of highly qualified audit companies to carry out the audit process. The ICTI CARE Foundation currently uses seven qualified audit firms that have undergone a rigorous technical review and approval process. They perform audits in accordance with ICP protocols primarily in China, with some occasional auditing in Macau, Hong Kong, Taiwan, Thailand, Vietnam, Indonesia and India. These audit firms have collectively performed hundreds of thousands of social compliance audits for ICTI CARE and their other clients across a broad range of multi-stakeholder, industry and brand ethical sourcing programs.

• Toy-producing factories register in the ICTI CARE Process to begin their progress toward certification that will qualify them to supply manufactured goods to brands, retailers and licensors that have committed their companies to source their products from ethical suppliers.

• To begin, they complete an application package. Once a factory's application has been accepted, Operations randomly assigns an audit firm from the list of seven qualified firms to conduct an unannounced audit.

• Once the audit firm issues a favorable report, the factory will receive a certification seal, valid for one year, after which it will be subject to another, unannounced audit. .

• If the audit firm issues a report that identifies any faults, the factory will be required to adopt a Corrective Action Plan to address them. Thereafter, a scheduled re-audit is done to ensure that the Corrective Action Plan has been implemented. Factories may be put on probation pending correction of identified faults.

• If the audit firm issues a report that identifies significant, critical faults, such as employment of underage or forced labor, or if a factory fails to demonstrate a commitment to correcting identified non-critical faults through adoption and implementation of a corrective action plan, factories may be terminated.

• The ICTI CARE Process has an extensive training program focused on helping workers to understand their rights and helping management to operate more effectively, using the Code of Business Practices as a guide to how to improve margins by improving the productivity of their workers through motivation and fair treatment.

Complaint Procedures:

Complaints about factory operations, policies or treatment of workers come to us in a variety of ways.

• First, one of the best sources is our confidential, worker Helpline—a free telephone and e-mail service that allows workers to ask questions of any kind. Very often they want to better understand their labor rights; but the service also serves as an avenue for complaints about the way they are being treated or the way the factory is run. The Helpline is manned by the Little Bird organization, a Chinese NGO specializing in labor issues. They answer routine questions directly and refer any serious matters (about 10% of the total) to our Operations team, which can intervene with factory management to seek resolution.

• Second, we receive direct communications to Operations, by e-mail or telephone, which we also investigate.

• Third, we are contacted by worker-focused NGOs. There are several with whom we have working relationships.

• Finally, some complaints also come during private interviews with workers that are a normal part of audits. Those complaints are incorporated in the audit report.

We take allegations seriously. Once we have received a complaint, we begin engaging directly with the parties involved.

• First, we compare the allegations received with how the factory fared in its most recent audit, including any Corrective Action Plan that the factory may have adopted.

• Second, our own staff auditors conduct an unannounced investigative audit. If necessary we can also use one of the seven qualified audit firms, but, as a matter of policy, we do not use the same firm that conducted the most recent audit.

• Based on the results, a report is prepared, comparing the allegations made by the complainant with what we found.

• Depending on the nature of the results, we may require a corrective action plan, place the factory on probation or terminate it.

• We will then publish our own report addressing the issues outlined by the complainant's report.

This process works best when we can work with the NGO from the beginning. This is often the case, including with earlier complaints lodged by China Labor Watch. We have even engaged CLW to verify issues found through our factory audits. They have done this by interviewing workers outside the factory. Then we compared their findings with ours, in what proved to be a very useful collaboration.

Working privately prior to publication of a report is almost always more productive than trying to correct issues after one is released. When a report becomes public, factory owners and managers may become more inclined to obscure actual conditions in order to present a better picture than what exists. But in a less pressured situation, factory owners may be more open to revealing actual problems, root causes and sustainable fixes. Given that the goal is to help workers, then all of the stakeholders should be brought together in a constructive manner to identify issues and solutions. Publishing a report is effective at gaining attention for the report issuer but is not always the most effective way to promote improvement in working conditions.

The ICP provides other services beyond auditing. we don't just investigate and require correction; we also help workers and factories to reach agreement on issues that arise between them.

An example of this, one that is in process right now, involves a factory that is closing down and moving to another location. Management planned to fire all the workers at the current site, but allegedly did not follow government-mandated procedures. So the workers went on strike. We were alerted to the situation almost simultaneously by Helpline calls and by a Hong Kong based NGO with which we have worked in the past: Working with them, factory management, worker leadership, government authorities and the toy brands involved, we have begun a mediation which we expect will be concluded successfully by next week.

The ICTI CARE Process was developed as an industry-wide approach to promote ethical manufacturing of toys and other children's products. With the support of a multi-stakeholder Board, a committed Operations team, experienced social compliance auditors, responsible brands and retailers supporting the process, toy manufacturers voluntarily choosing to undergo our process, and with the engagement of workers themselves, we have helped to improve the awareness and realization of better working conditions in toy factories in China and elsewhere. We have learned a lot in the past 10 years and we use what we have learned to constantly improve our processes. But, we recognize that our work is continuous and we have much work ahead of us.

Thank you for allowing us this opportunity to testify before the Commission today.

William S. Reese

Bill Reese was appointed President and Chief Executive Officer of the International Youth Foundation in 2005, having joined IYF in May 1998 as its Chief Operating Officer. He was President and CEO of Partners of the Americas for twelve years. Previously, he served with the Peace Corps for ten years, first as a volunteer in Salvador, Brazil, then as director of Brazil operations, and in Washington as deputy director of the Latin American and Caribbean region. He currently sits on the board of The Prince's Youth Business International in the UK as well as Inter-Action, where he served previously as Chair. Mr. Reese has also joined the Alcatel-Lucent Foundation Board and serves as a board member of two organizations committed to certifying best practices in global supply chains in the apparel and toy industries: W.R.A.P. and ICTI Care Foundation. Reflecting his interest in promoting international volunteerism, he has joined the boards of Encore International Service Corps and Global Citizen Year. Mr. Reese received his BA in Political Science from Stanford University and is a 1995 graduate of the Business School's Executive Program.

The International Youth Foundation

HTTP://WWW.IYFNET.ORG/

The International Youth Foundation (IYF) prepares young people to be healthy, productive, and engaged citizens.

For over twenty years, IYF has sought to tell a new story about the role of young people in our world. Rather than view youth as 'problems to be solved,' we recognize and support their role as creative problem solvers. We engage young people as partners in development, equipping them with the know-how and tools to contribute to their communities.

At the core of our work is creating new possibilities for young people.

We are passionate in our belief that educated, employed, and engaged young people possess the power to solve the world's toughest problems. Every young person therefore deserves the opportunity to realize his or her full potential. Our programs are catalysts for change that help youth learn, work, and lead.

Recognizing that no one sector of society alone has the resources or expertise to effectively address the myriad challenges facing today's youth, IYF is mobilizing a global community of businesses, governments, and civil society organizations—each committed to developing the power and promise of young people. Since 1990, IYF has mobilized over US$200 million in resources to expand the opportunities for the world's youth by helping to fund programs and partnerships with 472 youth-serving organizations worldwide. In 2013, our global network included 224 partners in 70 countries.

————

PREPARED STATEMENT OF EARL V. BROWN, JR.

DECEMBER 11, 2014

THE ENVIRONMENT FOR "SOCIAL AUDITING" IN THE PRC

The April 24, 2013 Rana Plaza factory collapse in Dhaka, Bangladesh, with its death toll of over 1,100 workers, and an abundance of evidence of negligence and indifference on the part of multi-national brands, manufacturers and building owners, poses a stark and tragic challenge to those that assert that international brands and other multinationals are able to effectively police compliance along the labyrinths of their supply chains with even the most elemental norms of occupational health and safety. The Rana Plaza disaster involved clear departures from the most common sense and simple standards of load bearing in building codes, and evacuation procedures.

The Rana Plaza structure had more than the permitted stories, and could not bear its additional illegal weight. After huge cracks appeared in pillars and walls, workers were pressured to remain at work under supervisory assurances from their employers that nothing was wrong, and with threats of job loss.[1] As work continued fulfilling contracts for major European Union and North American brands, the Rana Plaza building buckled and fell on top of thousands of workers. To date, the families of the dead, and the injured workers have not received anything like adequate compensation from any of the many wrongdoers who contributed to this outrage.[2]

The Rana Plaza collapse illustrates a fundamental flaw in the claim that multinational corporations are able to self-enforce even the most basic occupational health and safety codes. A current, empirically grounded scholarly assessment of corporate social responsibility (CSR) and social auditing, by Professor Richard M. Locke, makes only a most modest and contingent claim for CSR programs, including social auditing:

> . . . Private initiatives aimed at improving labor standards can succeed when global buyers with their suppliers establish long term, mutually beneficial relations and when various public institutions help to support these . . . relations . . .[3]

In short, absent public, governmental pressure, including state enforcement of corporate, business and labor laws, voluntary corporate policing does not yield much good, and overlooks much evil—as Rana Plaza demonstrates.

Indeed, any independent auditing of the behavior of manufacturers along supply chains depends on clear, comprehensive public legal and regulatory frameworks that establish standards and require basic reporting by manufacturers of compliance with those standards. To "audit" at all, much less to initiate "social audits," global brands and their lawyers and accountants must be able to investigate public and private records, as well as gather testimony and evidence to establish the facts of compliance or non-compliance with laws and policies. China presents many questions at even this threshold auditing step. This issue—whether China's environment

---

[1] Hossain, Farid. "Bangladesh: Owners' Many Failings Led to Collapse". *Associated Press.* 23 May 2013. Web. http://bigstory.ap.org/article/bangladesh-owners-many-failings-led-collapse

[2] The Rana Plaza Arrangement. "Rana Plaza Arrangement. Understanding for a Practical Arrangement on Payments to the Victims of the Rana Plaza Accident and their Families and Dependents for their Losses". 20 Nov. 2013. Web. http://www.ranaplaza-arrangement.org/mou/fulltext/MOU_Practical_Arrangement_FINAL-RanaPlaza.pdf

[3] Locke, Richard M. *The Promise and Limits of Private Power: Promoting Labor Standards in a Global Economy.* Cambridge: Cambridge UP, 2013. Print. p. 17.

allows any credible auditing—is one often openly discussed by business and regulators.[4]

Here is a summary list of the major problems of auditing in China:

- Public records concerning corporate identity are often difficult to access in the many jurisdictions of China, and are often not complete and/or accurate. The brands, far removed, often do not know who may be subcontracting from their prime contractors to fill accelerated "just-in-time" orders, and cannot even (after-the-fact) ascertain the identities of all employers in these complex supply chains. This opacity is most acute where there is child, prison or forced labor in a supply chain.
- Just "which" employer or business entity is responsible for compliance with labor and environmental laws is often in doubt due to a "hugger-mugger" of corporate entities and names that proliferate without much economic rationale precisely to disguise responsibility.[5] Workers often do not know the real identity of their legal employer.
- Manufacturers in labor intensive sectors like garments or toys often do not accurately report hours of work, pay and occupational health and safety matters, and are not pressed to do so by the authorities.[6]
- The brands themselves indirectly promote a business and regulatory environment in which labor laws and other social laws are not taken seriously by government or employers, with the result that social laws are not rigorously enforced. Local authorities often collude with or allow local employers to evade standards. In the absence of autonomous grassroots worker organizations to pressure supply chain employers to follow wage and hour laws, and other labor standards, employers who comply with the law end up at a competitive disadvantage with employers who avoid standards and thus produce product cheaper. This failure to enforce law evenly sets up fierce economic incentives to flout the law, with acquiescence by local government obsessed with growth targets. Brands often exacerbate this corrosive process. As Professor Locke found:

> Suppliers are asked to invest in improved labor and environmental conditions but are pressured to (and rewarded for) producing ever-cheaper goods . . .[7]

- Auditing firm staff are too often wholly ignorant of the context of industrial relations to know how to interview workers (if workers are even interviewed). In particular, the often junior and inexperienced audit staff relegated to labor auditing cannot begin to engage in the type of sensitive social investigation required to put workers at ease, and to prompt candid and truthful responses from workers. To the contrary, these auditors follow a rote checklist that workers fear must be answered the "right" way to avoid retaliation.[8]
- It takes time and considerable effort for independent worker rights advocates to establish the quality of relationship with industrial and service sector workers in China that permits candid discussions of working conditions. Many of the occupational health and safety practices in factories, mills, mines and transport hubs are appalling. Without some attempt to establish a more organic relationship with rank-and-file workers, auditors simply will not be able to assess whether safety and health standards are being maintained in factories and other work sites—assuming, of course, that the law and regulations are sufficiently developed to yield the comprehensive set standards required to set the framework for safe and healthy workplaces in many industrial environments.
- Corporate management often is compelled to engage law firms and investigators to uncover wrongdoing in its ranks or along supply chains when regular auditing is not sufficient. Yet, China recently imprisoned the principals of a long established investigation firm that had for years conducted corporate investigations unimpeded. Basically, the two lead investigators were convicted and imprisoned under a strained interpretation of Article 253 of China's Amendments to Criminal Law (VII) for "stealing or illegally obtaining, by any means,

---

[4] Lynch, Sarah. "SEC Judge Bars 'Big Four' Chna Units for Six Months Over Audits". *Reuters.* 23 Jan 2014. Web. http://www.reuters.com/article/2014/01/23/us-sec-china-bigfour-idUSBREA0L28D20140123

[5] United Mine Workers v. Coronado Coal Co., 259 U.S. 344, 411 (1922). (Chief Justice Taft's describing an employer's "attempt to evade his obligation by a hugger-mugger of his numerous corporations . . .")

[6] Locke supra at 36, observing that factory management often engages "in a cat and mouse game in which auditors uncover fabricated documents . . ."

[7] Locke, supra, at p. 35.

[8] Locke, supra, at 36–37.

personal information." [9] Where transparency is lacking, resorting to experienced lawyers and investigators is often necessary for corporate management to assess whether laws or commitments are being violated. Even more so in an opaque environment like China's. Now, lawyers, investigators and social scientists looking at wrongdoing along supply chains face the threat of criminal prosecution and even prison if their inquiries threaten the interests of those violating the law or corporate policy. Frankly, these prosecutions—against the backdrop of intense security over labor issues—undermine the endeavor of social auditing.

The validity of social auditing depends on its independence. CSR programs with a high degree of independence and participation by autonomous labor organizations and networks, such as the Worker Rights Consortium and the Accord [10] in Bangladesh, can contribute much to enforcing labor standards even in the absence of governmental pressure to abide by labor standards. Yet, staging supply chain compliance without sustained robust pressure by grassroots workers and their networks in China will ultimately prove to be akin to staging Hamlet without the Prince of Denmark.

———

PREPARED STATEMENT OF BRIAN CAMPBELL

DECEMBER 11, 2014

Thank you, Chairmans Brown and Smith for providing me the opportunity to share some ideas for tools the U.S. Government can employ that will help bring an end to the terrible abuses facing factory workers in China and in other countries.

As was well documented in China Labor Watch's report and testimony, though sweatshops are the result of complex, modern business practices by Multi-National Enterprises (MNEs), the reasons sweatshops exists are not complicated. Sweatshops are the result of high-stakes, intense cost and production pressures placed on local companies by multi-national enterprises. Unfortunately, during peak production season, the demands of the buyer can lead directly to coercive management policies, and, in many cases, forced labor to meet production demands. For example, in the case of Mattel Electronics Dongguan and Zhongshan Coronet factories, CLW documented how workers who initially voluntarily [1] came to work for the company eventually found themselves unable to leave during the peak season without having to leave behind wages they were already legally owed. International law and U.S. law prohibit any person, including companies and MNEs, from exacting labor from any person "under the menace of a penalty" and "for which they did not offer themselves voluntarily." Faced with the prospect of losing more than a month's wages, which is often the difference between dire poverty and making ends meet, some workers will simply walk away; others grudgingly accept that they have no choice but to keep working or lose their already hard earned pay. Migrant workers are particularly vulnerable, as they also risk losing their social insurance payouts, pensions, and health insurance payouts if forced to return to their home province. For many others, the menace of management's wrath and the loss of their wages lead to total loss of hope and suicide. In all situations, while the initial decision to work making, assembling, or packaging toys for MNEs such as Mattel was voluntarily, this voluntary labor was transformed into more sinister labor during the peak season in order to meet the contractual demands established by the buyers.

———

[9] Dentons. "Conducting compliance investigations in China: A new regulatory environment." 28 Aug 2014. Web. http://www.dentons.com/en/insights/alerts/2014/august/28/conducting-compliance-investigations-in-china-a-new-regulatory-environment

[10] Both the Worker Rights Consortium and the Accord are binding agreements to enforce labor standards with robust trade union participation.

Worker Rights Consortium. "The Designated Suppliers Program—Revised". 17 Feb. 2012. Web http://www.workersrights.org/dsp/DSP%20Program%20Description,%202012.pdf

As of this date, the Accord has been signed by 186 apparel companies from Europe, America, Asia and Australia, two global unions (IndustriALL and UNI Global Union), eight Bangladeshi trade union organizations, and four campaign organizations (Worker Rights Consortium, International labor Rights Forum, Clean Clothes Campaign and Maquila Solidarity Network).

The Accord on Fire and Building Safety in Bangladesh. "Official Signatories." Bangladesh Accord. 9 Dec 2014. Web. http://www.bangladeshaccord.org/signatories/

Also see the testimony given by Scott Nova of the Worker Rights Consortium to: US Senate Committee on Foreign Relations "Prospects for Democratic Reconciliation and Workers' Rights in Bangladesh." 11 Feb 2014. Web. http://www.foreign.senate.gov/hearings/prospects-for-democratic-reconciliation-and-workers-rights-in-bangladesh. In China, few worker rights organizations are part of the auditing process or CSR programs.

[1] ILO Convention No. 29.

With such dire consequences for workers, it is vital that the U.S. and Chinese government work closely together using all the tools at their disposal to bring an end to the root causes these labor abuses. In doing so, it is important that we remember two immutable facts that must inform any course of action.

First, unless workers can access a legally-biding remedy, they stand to lose if they raise complaints, use grievance processes, or take other actions to protect their rights. As is clearly demonstrated in China Labor Watch's report, workers are the most vulnerable person in the supply chain; they are simultaneously unable to protect themselves from management retaliation and from the economic hit caused by loss of business when companies use CSR policies incorporated into supplier contracts to rescind the contracts.

Second, Global Multi-national Enterprises and the companies that comprise them, like Mattel and Fisher-Price, exist by virtue of a grant of authority from governments and legislatures like our Congress, which endowed them with one overarching legal duty defining the very nature of the corporate "person's" character: a fiduciary duty to maximize profits on behalf of shareholders. As a result, business practices employed by companies like Mattel, such as lean production times and CSR programs, are designed primarily to achieve the singular legal duty to protect shareholders interests, even if other ancillary benefits may result from time to time. Viewed through this lens, it is no surprise that workers are treated as commodities, and high wages are viewed as a threat to MNEs everywhere.[2]

In order to strike a new balance between the myopic, profit-maximizing nature of the corporate "person" and the human beings impacted by their business practices, the U.S. and Chinese governments have already taken an important step by endorsing the United Nations Guiding Principles on Business and Human Rights. In line with OECD Guidelines for Multi-national Enterprises, the Guiding Principles provide a mutual framework for addressing human rights violations in global supply chains that cross national borders that are based on three core principles. First, governments have a duty to protect human rights by ensuring the fulfillment of "fundamental freedoms"[3], which include freedom from forced labor; Second, MNEs have a responsibility to respect human rights and *all* "applicable laws"[4], which are, significantly, enforceable in courts; Third, victims, such as exploited migrant workers, have a right to a meaningful, "effective" remedies.[5]

However, in order to implement the "respect, protect, and remedy" framework, Congress must pass necessary laws and regulations, including amending already existing legislation, to reflect these principles and ensure that effective remedies are in place for victims. And every agency of the U.S. government must take on their share of this work. This includes such agencies as the Securities and Exchange Commission, which is partly responsible for ensuring corporations fulfill their legal duties to shareholders, and the Department of Homeland Security, which ensures that companies in violation of labor laws like the prohibition against forced labor, do not profit from those crimes.

First, Congress must ensure that all companies, including companies under contract by the Department of Defense or the State Department to supply video games, toy games, and other electronics, are prevented from importing goods made with forced labor into the United States. Currently, the Tariff Act of 1930 prohibits the importation of goods made with forced labor, however most products made outside of the United States are exempt from the law because they are not also made domestically in sufficient quantities to meet consumptive demand. As a priority, Congress must remove the "consumptive demand exception," to the Tariff Act of 1930, which is a significant hurdle to enabling the Department of Homeland Security to work with their Chinese counterparts on bringing an end to the routine use of forced labor during peak production times, as described in the China Labor Watch report. When doing so, DHS must also update its regulations and procedures to improve internal coordination between Immigration and Customs Enforcement, which investigates the crime, and Customs and Border Protection, which enforces the law at the port.

[2] Bama Athreya and Brian Campbell. "No Access to Justice: the Failure of Ethical Labeling and Certification Systems for Worker Rights", in *Workers' Rights and Labor Compliance in Global Supply Chains: Is Social Label the Answer?*, ed. Jennifer Bair et al. (Routledge 2013).
[3] United Nations Guiding Principles on Business and Human Rights, General Principles. Accessed December 2014: http://www.ohchr.org/documents/publications/GuidingprinciplesBusinesshr_en.pdf
[4] Ibid.
[5] Ibid.

Second, Congress should pass H.R. 4842—Business and Supply Chain Transparency Act.[6] This important piece of legislation is a vital first step toward ensuring that MNEs implement their responsibility to respect, or "do no harm", by legally mandating companies to report on their diligence requirements, to include clear remedies for communities and populations impacted by a company's business practices.

Third, as the largest consumer of goods in the world, the U.S. Government must enact strong protections for its own supply chains to ensure that tax dollars do not support sweatshops and, if they are found to do so, that companies provide *effective, legally enforceable* remedies to victims. Soon, the Obama Administration will be issuing new, stronger procurement regulations requiring certain companies that supply goods to U.S. government contractors to abide by compliance plans in order to prevent *as well as* remedy any abuses.[7] It is important that Congress ensure that the Obama Administration issue the final regulations and that when implemented, the regulations will provide our government the tools necessary to stop not only forced labor but also sweatshop conditions and other business practices often accompanying or enabling forced labor.

Fourth, Congress must ensure that the U.S. Department of State's National Contact Point for the OECD Guidelines has the mandate and the resources to fully implement the recommendations of the NCP's Stakeholders Advisory Board, which are necessary to ensure the office is providing effective mediation and other forms of dispute resolution when requested through complaints brought by victims of human rights abuses caused by business practices of U.S. Multi-national Enterprises.[8]

Finally, it is vital that Congress work closely with human rights victims, their advocates, the business community, and the President toward the administration's goal that was announced this past September to build a comprehensive National Action Plan of laws, regulations, policies, and programs that to implement the UN Guiding Principles and the OECD Guidelines.

———

PREPARED STATEMENT OF HON. SHERROD BROWN, A U.S. SENATOR FROM OHIO;
CHAIRMAN, CONGRESSIONAL-EXECUTIVE COMMISSION ON CHINA

DECEMBER 11, 2014

Today is the last hearing for this Congress. It has been an honor to chair this Commission with my counterpart Congressman Chris Smith, over these last three and a half years. I want to thank our other Commissioners for their participation and support. Finally, the great work of this Commission would not have been possible without our incredible staff.

It is fitting that we end this year on an issue that hits so close to home this holiday season.

As parents, grandparents, aunts, and uncles, we care deeply about the toys we buy our children. We care about their safety. And we should care about who makes these toys.

It used to be the case that toys were made in America, in proud towns across this country.

Towns like Bryan, Ohio, where for 40 years, workers at the Ohio Art Company made Etch A Sketch, a toy many of us played with as kids.

In Bryan, the company was a family. Etch A Sketch was the town mascot.

But then Walmart told the company that in order keep its business they would need to sell the product for less than $10. And so what did Ohio Art do? In 2001, they moved production of Etch A Sketch to Shenzhen, China. A hundred people lost their jobs. A community lost its pride.

Today, some 85 percent of our toys come from China.

They will be made by factory workers like the ones investigated in China Labor Watch's most recent report.

Some of them are temp workers or students, making as little as $1.23 an hour and working more than 100 hours of overtime a month, in blatant violation of China's overtime laws.

They live in crowded dorms, as many as 18 people to a room. They stand for long hours at work. Emergency exit doors are locked.

---

[6] H.R.4842—Business Supply Chain Transparency on Trafficking and Slavery Act of 2014, Accessed December 2014: https://www.congress.gov/bill/113th-congress/house-bill/4842/text
[7] Proposed Rule. 78 FR 59317 (September 23, 2013).
[8] Report of the U.S. State Department Stakeholders Advisory Board (SAB) on Implementation of the OECD Guidelines for Multinational Enterprises, February 24, 2014. Accessed December 2014: http://www.state.gov/e/eb/adcom/aciep/rls/225959.htm

At the base monthly wage they are making, it would take nearly two months for one of these workers to afford the Thomas the Train mountain set that sells for $400 and is made in China.

We've seen this story repeated over and over again – American companies moving production to China to take advantage of cheap labor and poor labor enforcement and then resell these goods back to the United States. This business model is unprecedented in human history.

Eight years ago I introduced the Decent Working Conditions and Fair Competition Act to expand the Tariff Act of 1930 to prohibit the importation of goods made with sweatshop labor. But private industry said it didn't need a law, that members could deal with the problem on their own through codes of conduct, certifications, and audits. But eight years later, the problem hasn't gone away.

What I want to know today is, are corporate codes and self-policing sufficient, or do we need a new approach?

Does the toy industry in China need something like the legally-binding Bangladesh Accord, which I urged companies like Walmart and Target to join last year, or an anti-sweatshop law like the one I introduced eight years ago?

Something must be done. We need to be able to tell our children that the person who made their toys—perhaps the mother or father of another child—worked in a good place where she made a decent living.

We can't say that now.

I look forward to hearing from our witnesses and turn it over to my co-chair Congressman Smith for his statement.

———

PREPARED STATEMENT OF HON. CHRISTOPHER SMITH, A U.S. REPRESENTATIVE FROM NEW JERSEY; COCHAIRMAN, CONGRESSIONAL-EXECUTIVE COMMISSION ON CHINA

DECEMBER 11, 2014

Thank you, Chairman Brown, for calling this hearing and for your leadership the past two years as Chairman of the CECC. Your leadership has made this bipartisan Commission an effective one. You came to the Commission primarily interested in trade issues (we share those concerns). But I have noticed you taking a greater interest in human rights issues more broadly this past year, recognizing that U.S. interests in issues like food safety, fair trade, the environment, and regional security depend on human rights improvements in China. It has been an honor working with you.

I would like to welcome our witnesses and thank them for agreeing to testify today.

As Americans head to the stores this holiday season it is important to lift the curtain on an industry that has a history of labor problems. Last year, Americans bought an estimated $22 billion in toys, 80 percent of them made in China. The American consumer has a right to know how these toys are made and weigh the true costs of buying toys made in China.

This Commission has for several years documented the appalling state of working conditions and worker rights in China. In its most recent Annual Report, the Commission found that China continued to violate the basic human rights of its own people and seriously undermine the rule of law. Workers in China are still not guaranteed, either by law or in practice, fundamental worker rights in accordance with international standards.

The toy industry has had its share of labor problems, despite efforts to address these problems with voluntary codes and "social auditing," there continue to be serious problems. As our witnesses today will attest, Chinese workers are routinely exposed to a variety of dangerous working conditions that threaten their health and safety.

The deplorable state of worker rights in China hurts U.S. workers as well, by giving profoundly unfair advantages to those corporations who benefit from China's poor labor practices. The pursuit of lower and lower cost goods places tremendous pressure on factories to cut corners on worker pay and safety in order to remain competitive.

What are the human costs and economic consequences of this global race to the bottom of the cost curve? Are toy brands doing an adequate job in monitoring working conditions in their supply chain or is something else needed to ensure labor rights? As good corporate citizens, shouldn't toy companies ensure that international labor standards are being implemented in their factories?

I am also interested in answers to these questions and other issues of labor rights. This year I introduced with Representative Carolyn Maloney a bill that seeks to limit products made globally through forced or child labor. The Business Supply Chain Transparency on Trafficking and Slavery Act would require companies to describe measures they are taking to identify and address forced labor, human trafficking, and child labor in their supply chains. The use of forced and child labor continues to exist within the toy industry in China and as consumers we all have the right to know whether or not we are buying such items.

Again, Mr. Chairman, thanks for your leadership on this Commission and I look forward to working with you in the next Congress.

SUBMISSION FOR THE RECORD

_____

**ICTI CARE Process Response to China Labor Watch's November 18, 2014
Report on Five Toy Factories**

DECEMBER 18, 2014

This provides the ICTI CARE Foundation's[1] response to allegations raised by China Labor Watch (CLW) in its recently-issued report on its investigation of five toy factories in China. It is based on a thorough investigation of the allegations.

Summary

ICTI CARE takes seriously any concerns raised from any source regarding working conditions in ICTI CARE certified facilities. As part of our normal process, whenever complaints are voiced, we promptly and thoroughly investigate each allegation. This procedure involves a careful review of the most recent prior audits of the factories to determine if the alleged violations were present, and, if so, were the subject of a corrective action plan, followed by rigorous investigative audits conducted by our Quality Control team as well as outside auditors.

With respect to the recent claims made in China Labor Watch's November 18, 2014 report, we have completed audits of the facilities in the report and share the results of those here.

There was no support for a substantial majority, 67 out of 118, of the claims reported by CLW.

Three of CLW's 118 claims were validated and constituted actual violations. None of three violations were critical violations. The two factories immediately agreed to a corrective action plan to address those violations, and implementation of the corrective action plan will be verified in the next audit of those two factories.

Ten of CLW's claims were only partially validated. They often constituted simple documentation errors and the factories agreed to correct them at once. Again, the next audits of those factories will verify that they have done so.

The remaining 25 allegations made by CLW's report were supported but none of them constituted a violation of ICP's Code of Conduct and/or Chinese legal guidelines. For example:

- It is permissible under local legal requirements for workers to receive a copy of their contract a month after the commencement of their employment.
- Switching day and night shifts every two weeks violates neither ICP's Code of Conduct nor China's legal requirements.
- Some factories made copies of job applicants' personal IDs to conduct criminal background checks. That is understandable. No factory intentionally or illegally detained prospective workers' personal IDs.

Again, all of the factories agreed immediately to correct the few violations that were validated, and ICTI CARE will use its normal process to ensure that factories are living up to their commitments.

All of the investigative audits included documentation review, management interviews, visual inspects of the physical property, and worker interviews conducted in the absence of management. All five audits were unannounced and were scheduled as soon as possible after release of the CLW report.

ICTI CARE is always interested in ways to improve its processes and Code and will consider whether adjustments need to be made with respect to any of these issues. While there is always room for improvement—our Code of Conduct, for instance, is periodically reviewed and strengthened—ICTI Care even now is far better positioned to determine whether violations have occurred than CLW's undercover investigators.

Our trained auditors have access to factory records and all of the factory areas, the ability to interview management in depth, and the opportunity to interview workers selected by the auditors outside of the view of management. In fact these are aspects of all our audits.

In contrast, CLW's undercover workers are not trained auditors, and they interview only those workers who agree to an interview outside of the factory. The undercover workers, for example, have little to no access to management or to the factory's books and records. They accordingly have incomplete information that hampers their ability to assess reliably whether violations have actually occurred.

_____

[1] The ICTI CARE Foundation is a non-profit industry association, chartered in the State of New York and headquartered in New York City.

The ICTI CARE Foundation and Its Process

The ICTI CARE Foundation was created in 2004 as an ethical manufacturing initiative of the toy industry. It operates principally through an independent audit program, known as the ICTI CARE Process.[2]

ICP auditors independently monitor supplier performance to make sure they meet their responsibilities in the areas of health and safety, child and forced labor, working hours and wages, discrimination and disciplinary practices, and social benefits.

The auditors currently are drawn from seven qualified, independent audit firms that undergo a rigorous technical review and approval process every two years. As part of the audit process, they interview management and a sample of workers, they review the factory's books and records, and they inspect both the factory itself and factory-owned adjacent areas, such as dormitories and cafeterias.

The independent auditors issue a report for each factory. The audit report serves as the basis for recommendations from the auditors to the ICP on whether a factory has earned certification and, if so, its level of certification. Areas for improvement identified by the audit report are also the subject of a Corrective Action Plan adopted by the factory with the approval of the independent auditor.

Periodic re-audits are conducted to determine that a factory continues to qualify for certification, to determine whether the level of certification should be upgraded or downgraded, and to ensure that any past corrective action plan has been appropriately implemented.

The ICP is the core of our initiative. To date, thousands of independent factory audits have been conducted. Through November of this year alone, about 7,000 man-days of audits have been conducted.

Action Taken in Response to Complaints

Whenever complaints about a certified factory are received from any source—an e-mail, a call from our worker hotline, or an anecdotal report based on a non-governmental organization's undercover investigation-we conduct an audit that focuses on the substance of the complaint. This entails:

1. A thorough review of factory records to determine its current certification status and past audit results and corrective action plans.

2. An unannounced investigative audit of the factory, including interviews, examination of books and records, and visual inspections of facility premises.

3. Allowing client representatives to accompany our audit team to be able to observe (but not participate) in the audit.

4. A review of issues with factory management and establishing a Corrective Action Plan (CAP), as needed, during the audit exit interview.

5. Preparing an audit report with recommendations.

6. Following ICP management review, taking appropriate action (e.g., change certification level, place factory on probation or terminate it from the program, re-audits to ensure implementation of any corrective action plan, and so forth).

Conclusion

We take complaints about labor conditions in certified factories from any source seriously. Our record of placing factories on probation and terminating the certification of factories that are repeatedly non-compliant attests to this. These are not measures we take lightly, as they may have an effect on the factory's viability and on worker employment; however, such action may be necessary when facility management repeatedly fails to implement improvements.

Through our core ICP auditing program and corrective action process, as well as our Continuous Improvement Program and confidential worker hotline, we believe that we have helped achieve real progress in improving labor conditions at toy factories in China and elsewhere. We recognize that there is an opportunity for improvement and, as we have for years, we continue to invite CLW and other parties to work with us collaboratively to realize better working conditions in toy factories. For real, sustainable improvements to be made, it will require the constructive engagement of many parties—workers, factory managers, buyers and brands, social compliance auditors, civil society, governments, international institutions, consumers, and industry initiatives.

ICTI CARE Foundation
New York, December 18, 2014

○

---

[2] The ICTI CARE Process is the worldwide toy and children's products industries' ethical manufacturing program.

www.ingramcontent.com/pod-product-compliance
Lightning Source LLC
Chambersburg PA
CBHW080619180526
45168CB00007B/2976

9 781508 726517